CAN'T SLEEP
WRITE NOW

CAN'T SLEEP
WRITE NOW

a nocturnal journal for tireless thinkers

CHRONICLE BOOKS
SAN FRANCISCO

ISBN: 978-1-4521-0114-9

Manufactured in China

Designed by Shannon Losoreli

10 9 8 7 6 5 4

CHRONICLE BOOKS
680 Second Street
San Francisco, California 94107
www.chroniclebooks.com

INTRODUCTION

WHAT'S THE DIFFERENCE BETWEEN THE DAY AND NIGHT? There's the obvious—the day is generally bright and sunny, the night dark and mysterious. There are sounds, too—the boisterous cacophony of the day giving way to the lonesome chirping of crickets and rustling of branches. But one of the most important changes is how differently we think about the world during the day and night.

The daytime is for practical thoughts. Getting to work on time, finishing a project, deciding on lunch, scrambling to get home at a decent hour—between sunup and sundown our minds are busy making sense of our chaotic lives. Even our creative thoughts are moderated by the waking world, lending them a concrete structure and definite direction.

But something changes once the lights go down. Our daily cares and worries gradually fall away, leaving us relaxed and receptive. Routines that drive our waking life dissipate as we set a new course toward the small hours of the evening. It's then that our mental boundaries blur and interesting new perspectives begin to color our consciousness. For most of us, this nocturnal path leads naturally to sleep and the world of dreams. For writers, though, this is also a time of limitless possibilities. Released from the confines of the day, the mind springs to life, turning over unexpected new ideas, ensuring a sleepless and riveting night. Magical while they last, these detours eventually come to an end, either through exhaustion or with the first rays of dawn.

In the light of day, our nocturnal writings can seem amusing, poignant, or even bizarre. Regardless, keeping a record of these musings is an essential exercise for casual or even professional writers. What we jot down in the dead of night illuminates everything from our fondest wishes to our deepest fears. Meanwhile, it uncovers parts of our personality that might be hidden during the day, providing invaluable insight and revealing new depths of humor, compassion, or even anger. And for writers, nighttime thoughts offer a mother lode of rough-hewn gems ready to be polished into dazzling stories.

Use this journal as a guide for documenting all of your after-hours ruminations. Writing prompts are scattered throughout to help kick-start your imagination. Flip through the pages and pick a few that speak to you, or simply write down whatever comes to mind, using the included quotes as inspiration. Remember to keep this journal somewhere handy, like on your bedside table, for easy retrieval no matter what time you reach for it. Take a moment during the day to review what you've written—you might be surprised by what strange and intriguing thoughts come to you when you can't sleep.

"No small art is it to sleep. It is necessary to keep awake all day for that purpose."

FRIEDRICH NIETZSCHE

WHY CAN'T YOU SLEEP?

Fireworks Arcade

date _____
time

WHAT HAPPENED THE LAST TIME YOU STAYED UP ALL NIGHT?

date _____

time

date _____

time

THE NIGHT IS LIKE . . .

1

2

3

4

5

6

7

8

9

10

"Sleep is the most moronic fraternity in the world, with the heaviest dues and the crudest rituals."

VLADIMIR NABOKOV
SPEAK, MEMORY

date

time

date _____
time

date _____

time

date _____
time

ART IS FOR:

IS THERE EVER A GOOD REASON FOR FIGHTING?

date

time

date
time

date

time

date _____
time

"I often think that the night is more alive and more richly colored than the day."

VINCENT VAN GOGH

SHOULD I STAY OR SHOULD I GO?

date

time

date
time

WHAT HAVE YOU BEEN MEANING TO TELL YOUR PARENTS?

date

time

"Nighttime is really the best time to work. All the ideas are there to be yours because everyone else is asleep."

CATHERINE O'HARA

date

time

"Night is the mother of counsels."

GEORGE HERBERT

TIMING IS EVERYTHING, EXCEPT WHEN:

WRITE A REVIEW OF A STRANGE DREAM YOU HAD:

date _____
time

date _____
time

date _____
time

THIS IS WHERE DREAMS COME FROM:

"Night is the other half of life, and the better half."

JOHANN WOLFGANG VON GOETHE

WHAT IS THE BEST WAY TO GET TO KNOW A NEW CITY?

date _____
time

date _____
time

date _____
time

date _____
time

"One hour's sleep before midnight is worth two after."

ENGLISH PROVERB

INSTEAD OF COUNTING SHEEP, COUNT:

1

2

3

4

5

6

7

8

9

10

date _____
time

"Night, when words fade and things come alive."

ANTOINE DE SAINT-EXUPÉRY
FLIGHT TO ARRAS

WHAT WOULD YOU SPEND YOUR LAST DOLLAR ON?

CREATE A WORD TO DEPICT SOMETHING INDESCRIBABLE
AND WRITE ITS DEFINITION:

date _____

time

"The ideal reader suffers from an ideal insomnia."

JAMES JOYCE
FINNEGANS WAKE

REGRET TASTES LIKE THIS:

date

time

"I realize that from the cradle up I have been like the rest of the race—never quite sane in the night."

MARK TWAIN

YOU + LONG DRIVE =

date _____
time

"A ruffled mind makes a restless pillow."

CHARLOTTE BRONTË

WHEN DO YOU FEEL TRULY INTIMATE WITH SOMEONE?

date

time

date

time

"You never have to change anything you got up in the middle of the night to write."

SAUL BELLOW

DESCRIBE AN AWKWARD SITUATION, WRITING WITH YOUR
NONWRITING HAND:

A JOURNEY TONIGHT WOULD TAKE YOU HERE:

"Most glorious night! Thou wert not sent for slumber!"

LORD BYRON

INFINITY IS LIKE:

_____
_____
_____
_____
_____
_____
_____
_____
_____
_____
_____
_____
_____
_____
_____
_____
_____
_____

"The day has eyes, the night has ears."

SCOTTISH PROVERB

ARE WORDS JUST WORDS?

date _____

time

"Up, sluggard, and waste not life; in the grave will be sleeping enough."

BENJAMIN FRANKLIN

A RECIPE FOR THE PERFECT DISASTER WOULD INCLUDE:

1

2

3

4

5

6

7

8

9

10

"Night is the mother of thoughts."

JOHN FLORIO

THE LAST TIME YOU LAUGHED UNTIL IT HURT WAS:

_____

_____

_____

_____

_____

_____

_____

_____

_____

_____

_____

_____

_____

_____

_____

_____

date _____
time

date _____
time

A BOX THAT WOULD FIT ALL OF YOUR THOUGHTS
WOULD LOOK LIKE THIS:

WRITE YOUR OPERATING INSTRUCTIONS:

date _____

time

"A man may write at any time, if he will set himself doggedly to it."

SAMUEL JOHNSON

DARKNESS IS LIKE:

1

2

3

4

5

6

7

8

9

10

"It appears that every man's insomnia is as different from his neighbor's as are their daytime hopes and aspirations."

F. SCOTT FITZGERALD
THE CRACK-UP

WHEN YOU SAY "FINE," WHAT DO YOU REALLY MEAN?

date _____
time

WHERE IS THE BEST PLACE TO GO
TO LEARN MAGIC?

"Insomnia never comes to a man who has to get up exactly at six o'clock. Insomnia troubles only those who can sleep any time."

HARRY PERSONS TABER
THE PHILISTINE: A PERIODICAL OF PROTEST

date _____
time

date _____
time

"If you can't sleep, then get up and do something instead of lying there worrying."

DALE CARNEGIE

date _____
time

date _____

time

WRITE THE SHORTEST SHORT STORY EVER WRITTEN:

"I haven't been to sleep for over a year. That's why I go to bed early. One needs more rest if one doesn't sleep."

EVELYN WAUGH
DECLINE AND FALL

HOW DO YOU TURN OFF YOUR BRAIN?

date _____
time

IF LIFE IS LIKE A BOWL OF CHERRIES, LOVE IS LIKE:

"How do people go to sleep? I'm afraid I've lost the knack."

DOROTHY PARKER
THE LITTLE HOURS

SLEEPY IS LIKE:

1

2

3

4

5

6

7

8

9

10

WHAT HAPPENS AT THE END OF THE DREAM YOU HAVE MOST OFTEN?

date

time

"We use up too much artistic effort in our dreams; in consequence our waking life is often poor."

FRIEDRICH NIETZSCHE

date _____
time

date _____

time

"In a real dark night of the soul it is always three o'clock in the morning."

F. SCOTT FITZGERALD
THE CRACK-UP

WHAT ARE YOU AFRAID OF?

WILD ANIMALS ARE WILD BECAUSE:

_____

_____

_____

_____

_____

_____

_____

_____

_____

_____

_____

_____

_____

_____

_____

_____

"If a man had as many ideas during the day as he does when he has insomnia, he'd make a fortune."

GRIFF NIBLACK

DESCRIBE YOUR EXACT OPPOSITE:

_____

_____

_____

_____

_____

_____

_____

_____

_____

_____

_____

_____

_____

_____

_____

_____

_____

date

time

COZY SMELLS LIKE:

1

2

3

4

5

6

7

8

9

10

"Those no-sooner-have-I-touched-the-pillow people are past my comprehension. There is something bovine about them."

J. B. PRIESTLEY

DRAW WHERE YOU WOULD RATHER BE:

date

time

"Tomorrow night is nothing but one long sleepless wrestle with yesterday's omissions and regrets."

WILLIAM FAULKNER

DESCRIBE WHAT YOU SEE WHEN YOU CLOSE YOUR EYES:

_____

_____

_____

_____

_____

_____

_____

_____

_____

_____

_____

_____

_____

_____

_____

"Dawn: when men of reason go to bed."

AMBROSE BIERCE
THE DEVIL'S DICTIONARY

date _____
time

IMAGINE A CONVERSATION WITH A CAT OR DOG.
WHAT WOULD YOU ASK? HOW WOULD IT RESPOND?

"The repose of sleep refreshes the body. It rarely sets the soul at rest."

GASTON BACHELARD

"Early to rise and early to bed/Makes a man healthy and wealthy and dead."

JAMES THURBER

WHAT WOULD YOU DO WITH TOMORROW
IF TOMORROW WAS ALL YOU HAD?

WRITE THE LONGEST SENTENCE YOU CAN:

date _____
time

"There are twelve hours in the day and above fifty in the night."

MARIE DE RABUTIN-CHANTAL

date _____

time

THE MOON IS LIKE:

1

2

3

4

5

6

7

8

9

10

date _____
time

WHAT HAPPENS NEXT?

date _____
time

date

time

date _____
time

date _____

time

date

time

date _____

time

date _____
time

date

time

date _____

time

date

time

date _____
time

LATE-NIGHT MOVIE LIST:

SNACKS FOR SLEEPLESS NIGHTS:

MIDDLE-OF-THE-NIGHT BRILLIANT IDEAS:

_____

_____

_____

_____

_____

_____

_____

_____

_____

_____

_____

_____

_____

_____

_____

_____

_____

_____

NIGHTTIME READING LIST:

_____
_____
_____
_____
_____
_____
_____
_____
_____
_____
_____
_____
_____
_____
_____
_____
_____

NIGHTTIME ACTIVITIES (BESIDES WRITING):

PEOPLE TO CALL AFTER-HOURS:

LOCAL ALL-NIGHT BARS AND DINERS:

TRICKS FOR FALLING ASLEEP:

_____

_____

_____

_____

_____

_____

_____

_____

_____

_____

_____

_____

_____

_____

_____

_____

_____